MICHIGAN

SMITHMARK

This edition first published in 1992 by SMITHMARK
Publishers Inc., 112 Madison Avenue,
New York, New York 10016

ISBN 0-8317-0504-3

Printed and bound in Spain

Writer: Nancy Millichap Davies
Designer: Ann-Louise Lipman
Design Concept: Lesley Ehlers
Editor: Joan E. Ratajack
Production: Valerie Zars
Photo Researcher: Edward Douglas
Assistant Photo Researcher: Robert V. Hale
Editorial Assistant: Carol Raguso

Title page: Lake Superior's waters reflect a classic fishing boat in Copper Harbor at the tip of the Keweenaw Peninsula. *Opposite:* Detroit architecture, yesterday and today: Statuary atop Wayne County Courthouse (1902) contrasts with the bold lines of Renaissance Center. *Overleaf:* Seen from the Detroit River, the city's skyline and Ambassador Bridge, crossing to Windsor, Ontario, glitter beneath a spectacular full moon.

Above, left: Neon-edged beasts and logo above Detroit's Fox Theatre marquee date from cinema's glory days. *Right:* Under a mural's wild-eyed gaze, shoppers sample farm produce at the Eastern Market, which sold hay and wood when it opened in 1870. *Below:* A tiled wall identifies Trappers Alley, a contemporary urban mall in Greektown.

In the language of the Ojibway, the word *Michigan* means "great water." The name fits this state surrounded and shaped by the five Great Lakes, the world's largest group of inland waters. Three-quarters of Michigan, which borders all the Great Lakes but Lake Ontario, is bounded by water, and its total shoreline is longer than that of any state but Alaska. The lakes, and the rivers, such as the Grand and the Saginaw, which run from the state's interior into them, have been Michigan's vital arteries, and have defined the region's outlines, since before the Ice Age.

Along these waterways came the earliest Europeans to see the wild country that would one day become the twenty-sixth state. Michigan's story is the story of the changes wrought by those newcomers and all the others who followed, the towns and cities they built, the industries they founded.

It is also the story of those special places off the main thoroughfares of commerce that remain little changed today. The first European to explore the densely forested territory was Etienne Brulé, who arrived about 1620. He came along on Samuel de Champlain's search for trade routes to the Orient and was sent farther west than the main party. To explorers like Brulé, who was also hunting for furs to send home to France, Michigan—along with the nearby Canadian forests from which it was, at the time, indistinguishable—was a remote backwater of the vast region they called New France, more a route than a destination.

Top to bottom: Marshall Frederick's "Spirit of Detroit" (foreground) and high-rising Renaissance Center (background, right) express urban vitality. The fountain in Civic Plaza appears to dwarf Renaissance Center's glass towers in this shot. Larger than life, a boxer's arm is an emblem of power in the "Monument to Joe Louis," who, some say, was the greatest fighter ever.

The Jesuit priests who followed them regarded the region differently. They came as missionaries, bringing the Roman Catholic faith to the native people. In 1688, the most famous of them, Father Marquette, established the first permanent European settlement in the region, a mission at Sault Sainte Marie on the northern side of Michigan's Upper Peninsula.

For almost a century, Michigan remained a French frontier territory. No buildings from these early days of Gallic settlement remain because French construction methods involved inserting timbers directly into the earth, and these soon rotted. Yet Michigan place-names recall the era: Detroit, Au Sable, Isle Royale, and many others. And most of the French-speaking settlers remained after the British took over the administration of the territory in 1763. In fact, more than half of Michigan's European-descended population was French in background at least through 1820.

Since the days when Etienne Brulé and the other *voyageurs* who followed in his wake glided along the shores in fur-laden canoes, the lakes have helped Michigan become a hub of national and international trade despite its inland location. Transportation by water continues to be important for Michigan's products. The state's lakefronts and riversides are meccas for weekending Michiganians and the state's visitors.

Michigan's Upper Peninsula, which juts north and west across two of the Great Lakes, is more nearly surrounded by water than is the Lower Peninsula, the larger

At Heidelberg and Gratiot, streetwise art by Tyree Guyton combines the wheels of "Motor City" with signs, found objects, and brightly splashed paint.

Among the treasures in the Detroit Institute of Arts' spacious galleries are four murals depicting automobile production painted in the 1930's by Mexican artist Diego Rivera, one of which is pictured below. *Following pages, left:* White-hot molten steel rushes downward at a foundry in Detroit. *Right:* Sparks from an auto assembler's welding torch leave glowing trails.

Preceding page: Nineteenth-century buildings house up-to-the-minute shops and restaurants that attract visitors to Detroit's Greektown, one of the city's ethnic neighborhoods. *This page, above:* A museum for the pop music fan, Hitsville USA tells the story of Motown. The Detroit-born music style spread nationwide in the mid-1960's. *Below:* Baseball under the lights at Tiger Stadium.

Auto magnate Henry Ford founded the museum bearing his name in Dearborn, his home town. One focus of the collections: antique autos (below).

Related artifacts surround a 1950's Chevy in the Car Culture exhibit. *Below:* Cars on display in the museum's Automobile in American Life exhibit.

Above, left: A glockenspiel clock in Greenfield Village is part of Ford's museum complex in Dearborn. *Right:* Heinz House is one of 80-plus residences moved here to honor inventors and businessmen. *Below:* Visitors travel back in time behind a working steam engine.

portion of the state. It was added to the region that would become the state of Michigan in a political trade-off during the area's years as an American territory. The peninsula, which forms a barrier between Lake Superior and Lake Michigan was at that time, a remote area of deep forests and very little settlement. It remained so until the middle of the nineteenth century, when Americans began to mine a resource that the native Americans of the region had been exploiting for centuries: copper. Ores from which to smelt the red-gold metal are abundant in the Keweenaw Peninsula, a projection that points out into Lake Superior like a finger from the "hand" of the rest of the Upper Peninsula. Prospectors also discovered iron ore in the Keweenaw.

Entrepreneurs of the time faced the problem of delivering Upper Michigan's ores to more heavily settled areas south and east, where there were workers to smelt them. In 1855, the Soo Canal opened at Sault Sainte Marie. Its locks allowed cargo vessels to make the 22-foot drop from Lake Superior to Lake Huron. In the early 1900s this canal saw more shipping than either the Panama or the Suez canals. Copper and iron ore from the Upper Peninsula fueled the development of the iron and steel industry in the Ohio Valley and, later, the Lower Peninsula's auto industry.

Although some strip-mining of copper continues today, most onetime mining towns offer more historical than economic interest.

Top to bottom: One of Greenfield Village's numerous craft demonstrators, a potter, turns his wheel. Laboratory equipment of an earlier time gleams in a re-creation of Thomas Edison's Menlo Park Laboratory. Costumed employees tend hearth and spinning wheel in the village's Colonial-era saltbox house.

Dictionary author Noah Webster's New Haven, Connecticut, home is reconstructed in Greenfield Village. *Below:* Greenfield visitors board the Suwanee, a nineteenth-century paddlewheel steamboat.

Agricultural practices of the nineteenth century continue at the Firestone Farm in Greenfield Village.

Preceding page: A prototype of the Lunar Roving Vehicle, designed for moon surface travel (foreground), and a mock-up of Lunar Exploration Spacecraft Surveyor III (above) are at the Michigan Space Center in Jackson. *This page, above:* University of Michigan cheerleaders whoop it up at a football game against Ohio State. *Below:* Fans and alumni enjoy a pre-game tailgate picnic.

However, the Upper Peninsula's forests and lake shores increasingly serve as a rugged refuge for vacationing urbanites.

Between the Upper and Lower Peninsulas, islands dot the waters of Lakes Huron and Michigan. Especially popular with visitors is picturesque Mackinac Island, named by native Americans for the "giant turtle" that its limestone hump resembles. The stone ramparts of Fort Mackinac, once home to a British garrison and later an American military outpost until 1895, overlook the harbor on Lake Huron. The first Michigan resort to become widely known, Mackinac Island was attracting travelers by the 1830s. Rockers still line the 660-foot lakefront verandah of its 1887 Grand Hotel, the Middle West's showiest hostelry in the days of steamboat travel. Today, a ban on automobiles on the island enhances the nineteenth-century mood.

Just to the west of Mackinac Island, the Straits of Mackinac form the narrowest passage between Lakes Huron and Michigan. The water barrier posed an obstacle to easy travel between the two parts of the state until 1957, when a remarkable bridge joining the Upper and Lower Peninsulas was completed. The Mackinac Bridge, sometimes known as "Big Mac," is the longest total suspension bridge in the world, with a length of 8,614 feet from cable anchorage to cable anchorage.

Top: Shapes of the future: a geodesic dome and a Mercury Redstone launch vehicle at Jackson's Michigan Space Center. *Left:* At the Michigan Space Center, a space vehicle towers above a sign memorializing Gregory Jarvis, a Michigan native killed in the 1986 explosion of the space shuttle *Challenger.*

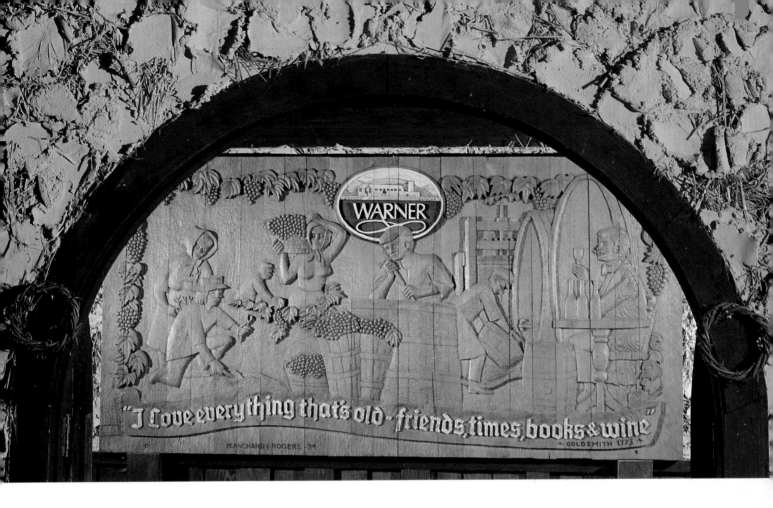

A wood plaque at Warner Vineyards in Paw Paw illustrates wine production and enjoyment. *Below:* Warner, the Midwest's largest winery, at harvest time.

Water was not the only barrier to travel in Michigan's early days. Early Michiganians faced a road-less interior covered with forests, except for a small area of open prairie in the extreme southwestern corner. Farmland was at its best there and along the state's western Lake Michigan shore, where fruit and vegetable cultivation continue to thrive today. Benton Harbor's fruit market has been called the world's largest, and Traverse City considers itself the "Cherry Capital of the World."

In the early years of statehood, most people in Michigan were farmers, living and growing crops where the land was good. The glacier-scoured, thin-soiled land of the Laurentian Shield, an ancient cap of granite that underlies the northern part of the state and much of Canada, was ill suited to crops but rich with unbroken stretches of pine forest. Logging those forests sustained Michigan's economy throughout the nineteenth century.

At the same time, manufacturing was getting under way. With lumber so close to hand, it was natural that furniture making became an important industry, with Grand Rapids the leading city in its production. Other enterprising manufacturers turned the readily available wood into wagons and carriages, paving the way for the automobile industry to come. Flint, the center of the carriage industry, was calling itself "Vehicle City" years before the first Buick rolled off a Flint assembly line.

Top: Sunset throws a lighthouse, people fishing, and a pleasure boat into sil-houette against the Lake Michigan horizon at St. Joseph. *Left:* A Great Lakes freighter dwarfs Benton Harbor's lighthouse.

Companions watch dusk settle on Lake Michigan from a Saugatuck lifeguard station.

The 1907 lighthouse at Holland Harbor on Lake Michigan is nicknamed "Big Red."

Many of Michigan's surviving historic homes were built during the nineteenth century for those who made their fortunes in the lumber business. The builders worked fine timber in high Victorian style. Some of the houses they created, such as the Hackley and Hume houses in Muskegon, are vast by today's standards. They are preserved in the historic districts of the Lower Peninsula towns that were once lumbering centers, such as Bay City's Center Avenue.

The height of Michigan lumber production was reached in 1888, when more than four billion board feet passed through its sawmills. The "Big Cut" continued until the state's forests were substantially cleared, and without timber the state's economy declined. But salvation, in the form of the Horseless Carriage, was at hand. The old French settlement of Detroit became the heart of the new economic boom. Its strategic location along the series of waterways that joins Lakes Huron and Erie gave Detroiters access to raw materials from the north and to markets in the south and east. The city already had carriage factories, but not far away, in what has since become the city of Dearborn, an immigrant Irish farmer's son named Henry Ford was tired of long, muddy wagon rides into town.

The city whose name came to stand for the auto industry has been Michigan's dominant urban center since the first century of European settlement. Like the rest of the Michigan territory, Detroit was marked out and named by French explorers.

Top: A drawbridge links Holland's Windmill Island to the mainland. *Right:* Holland residents brought De Zwaan Windmill from the Netherlands and reconstructed it in tribute to the town's Dutch heritage.

Grand Rapids is Michigan's second-largest city. The furniture manufacturing center was the home town of Gerald Ford.

The Gerald Ford Museum in Grand Rapids memorializes the thirty-eighth president's career. *Below:* Reflecting windows and terraced fountains give the museum entrance a spacious, airy effect.

In a barn near Grand Rapids, farm machinery awaits yet another growing season.

Haystacks and stubble alternate amid late-day shadows in an Iona County field after harvest.

Preceding pages: In this wintry Grand Haven State Park scene, lights along the pier leading out to Grand Haven Lighthouse parallel a band of sunset color on the Lake Michigan horizon. *This page, above:* On a Muskegon County beach, gentle waves catch the western light. *Below:* Snow fencing patterns a view of lakeside dunes.

Antoine de la Mothe Cadillac, looking to stem competition from English fur traders, established a new settlement in 1701 at the narrowest point of the strait joining Lake St. Clair and Lake Erie. He called it Fort Ponchartrain d'Etroit, combining the name of one of Louis XIV's ministers, Jerome Phelypeaux, Count de Pontchartrain, with the French term for "of the strait."

The town remained largely a French trading post until its takeover in 1764 by the British. The British also traded with native Americans for furs there and built Fort Lernoult during the Revolutionary War in an attempt to hold the strategic site. They finally ceded the city—and Michigan with it—to the fledgling United States in 1796. Detroit's role as an important center of trade continued throughout the nineteenth century.

Michiganians were active in the development of autos from the first decade of experimentation in the 1890s, but other states also had small car manufacturing centers at that time. Two innovations of the early twentieth century brought Detroit to the fore. Marketing mastermind William C. Durant formed General Motors, the country's first conglomerate, from a number of smaller auto companies. At about the same time, Henry Ford introduced the assembly line-produced Model T, making automobiles affordable for many middle-class people.

From World War I until the present, auto manufacturing has been the single most important industry in the Detroit area.

Top: Aglow with intense heat, steel pours into molds at a Muskegon foundry. *Right:* Dangerous energy streaks the air as engine blocks are cast in Muskegon.

An isolated Kent County barn is a midwestern classic in shape and color. *Below:* A Holstein dairy herd awaits the evening milking in Mason County. *Opposite::* Big Sable Point Lighthouse on Lake Michigan, Mason County, catches late-day sunlight.

Preceding page: The Michigan State Capitol Building (1879), in Lansing, reflects the prosperity that railroads and lumbering brought the state in the late nineteenth century. *This page, above left:* Glockenspiel Tower in Frankenmuth recalls the Bavarian ancestry of the community's settlers—as do the town's two breweries. *Right:* Frankenmuth's Bavarian Festival in June attracts many visitors to the town. *Below:* Life-size nativity figures greet shoppers year-round outside Bronner's Christmas Store in Frankenmuth.

Plants elsewhere in Michigan, especially in Saginaw, Flint, and Lansing, added to production. Workers from abroad and from within the United States, especially African-Americans from the South, migrated to Detroit for work. Their arrivals created a city with a multitude of ethnic groups, many of which concentrated in particular neighborhoods. The largest group arriving from abroad in the present century were Poles; Hamtramck (named for Colonel John Francis Hamtramck, the first American military commander of Detroit), the section of Detroit in which they settled, retains a Polish flavor. Detroit also has a sizable Greek community. The largest concentration of Arab immigrants in the United States lives in suburban Dearborn, where Lebanese coffeehouses and Syrian grocery stores give the neighborhood a Middle Eastern feeling.

The auto industry continues to dominate the city's manufacturing scene, but fewer Detroiters today work in factories than in service industries. And many of those who work in Detroit live in one of its widely sprawling suburbs. Flight to the suburbs accelerated after parts of downtown Detroit were damaged and demoralized by a 1967 riot. As the seventh-largest city in the U.S., Detroit remains an economic powerhouse, but the problems of inner-city poverty and physical deterioration are acute.

Top: Implements at the stagecoach stop in Irish Hills recall earlier methods of travel and commerce. *Left:* A super-market of the past, an old-time general store offers a colorful array of merchandise at the stagecoach stop in Irish Hills. *Opposite:* Early morning fog hangs over Otter Lake near Empire.

The 1871 lighthouse on South Manitou Island, part of the Sleeping Bear Dunes National Lakeshore, remained in use until 1958. *Below:* Visitors clamber up a sandy slope on the Sleeping Bear Dunes, which can reach 400 feet in height. *Opposite:* A lakeshore panorama from the vantage point of Empire Bluff, where bare branches mark a long-gone forest. .

A visitor to Sleeping Bear Dunes waves from the window of the 1857 Glen Haven Inn. *Below, left:* Rope coils form an intriguing design in a restored rescue surfboat displayed at Sleeping Bear Point Coast Guard Maritime Museum Boathouse. *Right:* A historic building in Glen Arbor houses an antique shop and attracts many visitors.

One response to the challenge is the Renaissance Center riverfront development in the heart of the city, a glittering complex that includes office buildings, a hotel, and a convention center that sprang into life in the 1970s.

The Detroit suburb of Dearborn houses Michigan's most popular historical attractions. In Greenfield Village, buildings from the nineteenth century have been re-assembled to recreate the life of that era. Together with the nearby Henry Ford Museum, this reconstruction not only presents visitors with information about bygone processes and products, but also captures the atmosphere of an era of rapid technological development that transformed the daily life of the entire nation. In Greenfield Village, for instance, stand Thomas Edison's laboratory from Menlo Park, New Jersey, where he perfected the light bulb, and the Dayton, Ohio, bicycle shop where Orville and Wilbur Wright built the first airplane.

While Dearborn's institutions preserve the aura of the late nineteenth century, the Cranbrook Educational Community further west in Bloomfield Hills pays tribute to the architectural styles of the early twentieth. Founded in the 1920s by newspaper publisher George Booth and his wife, Ellen Scripps Booth, the complex of day and boarding schools designed by distinguished Finnish architect Eliel Saarinen places a special emphasis on the arts and arts education. The schools surround the Booths' 1908 home, which was designed in the English manorial style by Detroit architect Albert Kahn. It houses the couple's extensive collections of American Arts and Crafts-style furniture and objects d'art.

Top: The emblem of the Leland Volunteer Fire Department, seen here on an old wooden door, once signified that the owner had paid for fire protection. *Right:* Leland was a commercial fishing center in the nineteenth century; today pleasure craft and fishing boats mingle at the waterside.

At 8,614 feet from cable anchorage to cable anchorage, the Mackinac Bridge (1957) linking Michigan's Upper and Lower peninsulas was the world's longest total suspension bridge when completed. *Opposite, top:* The 277-room Grand Hotel on Mackinac Island has been a famous lodging place since its 1887 opening. *Bottom:* Rocking chairs line the Grand Hotel's lakefront veranda, "the world's longest front porch" at 660 feet.

Detroit was the only incorporated city in the new state when Michigan was admitted to the Union in 1837. For the first decade, it was the capital. But the state legislature determined that the permanent capital should be more centrally located within the peninsula, especially at a time when its members feared that Detroit, just across the river from Canada, would be vulnerable in the event of another war with the British. Legislators from all over inland Michigan promoted their towns as potential capitals. Marshall even designated as "Capitol Hill" a site that retains the name to this day. Eventually an Ingham County landowner named James Seymour offered to donate 20 acres and put up buildings as large as those used for the capital at Detroit. Although the site was a wilderness, legislators who knew a bargain when they heard one took up his offer, and Lansing became the state's capital. After a slow start 1871 saw the coming of the railroad and, not long after, a domed, four-story Renaissance Revival capitol of white sandstone replaced the earlier wooden capitol. Turn-of-the-century industrial development centered around the automotive factories founded by pioneering inventor Ransom E. Olds. Reos, Stars, Durants, and Oldsmobiles rolled off Lansing assembly lines in the industry's early years, and Oldsmobiles continue to be made there.

Adjacent East Lansing is the home of Michigan State University, founded in 1855 as the first agricultural college in the country. Ann Arbor is another Michigan name with academic clout. The town, northwest of Detroit, has been the home of the nationally distinguished University of Michigan since 1841. Today it is a center of industrial research as well as of scholarship.

Immigrants to Michigan did not always settle in Detroit. The Upper Peninsula, for instance, has a substantial Finnish heritage. And in the southwestern part of the state, Dutch men and women fleeing religious persecution and

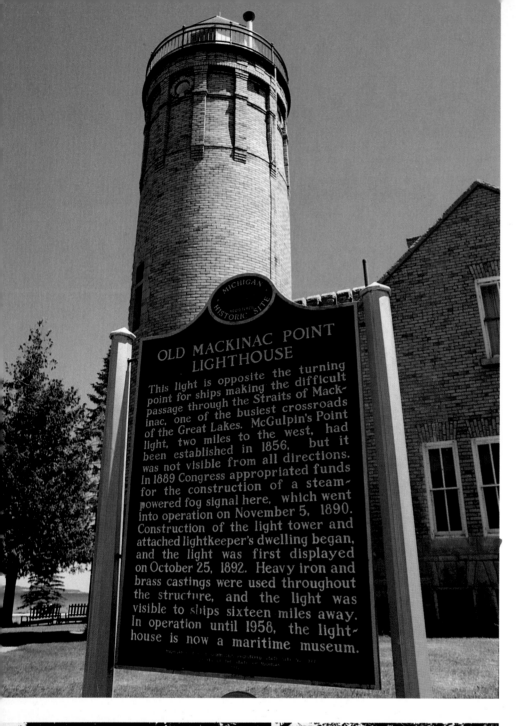

OLD MACKINAC POINT LIGHTHOUSE

This light is opposite the turning point for ships making the difficult passage through the Straits of Mackinac, one of the busiest crossroads of the Great Lakes. McGulpin's Point light, two miles to the west, had been established in 1856, but it was not visible from all directions. In 1889 Congress appropriated funds for the construction of a steam-powered fog signal here, which went into operation on November 5, 1890. Construction of the light tower and attached lightkeeper's dwelling began, and the light was first displayed on October 25, 1892. Heavy iron and brass castings were used throughout the structure, and the light was visible to ships sixteen miles away. In operation until 1958, the lighthouse is now a maritime museum.

famine founded the town of Holland in 1847. Every spring since 1929, hundreds of thousands of visitors have come to see the glowing expanses of flowers on display during Holland's Tulip Festival. In further tribute to their heritage, its citizens brought from the Netherlands the De Zwaan windmill and erected it in a riverside park.

Regions where people have not settled in substantial numbers, now being preserved with minimal development, give travelers some sense of that original, long-gone Michigan wilderness. Among the state's most distinctive wild regions is 45-mile-long Isle Royale, the largest island in Lake Superior, 15 miles northeast of the Keweenaw Peninsula. The federal government acquired the island from the Ojibway people in 1842 to establish copper mines, but Isle Royale's deposits were never particularly rich. Mining operations were abandoned by 1900.

In the twentieth century, the island's mountainous interior, dotted with lakes, and its coasts, lined with fine natural harbors, have lured nature lovers who take in its beauty by boat or on foot. The island's wildlife includes a moose herd that sometimes numbers up to 1,000 animals, and packs of wolves, rarely spotted by visitors, who prey on the moose and thus keep the population at a size the island can support. Hunting is prohibited. In 1940 Isle Royale became a national park, guaranteeing that generations to come will enjoy its unspoiled grandeur.

The federal government also protects two beautiful wild stretches of Michigan's extensive coastline as preserves for those who enjoy hiking, backpacking,

Top: The 1892 lighthouse at Mackinac's Maritime Place houses a historical museum. *Left:* Wearing uniforms that recall the fortress's heyday during the American Revolution, Fort Mackinac reenactors fire their rifles.

The Soo Locks at Sault Ste. Marie enable Great Lakes freighters to make the 22-foot drop from Lake Superior to Lake Huron. *Below:* Harsh Lake Superior weather has produced a colorful patchwork of peeled paint on these old fishing boats at Whitefish Point on Michigan's Upper Peninsula.

Sunset light brings out the subtle colors of the sandstone bluffs of Pictured Rocks National Lakeshore, on the Upper Peninsula in Alger County. *Below:* Hardy shore grasses bend gracefully in the winds that sculpt Pictured Rocks' shifting dunes.

Dead tree trunks rise from a sand dune, the ghostly remnants of a forest. *Below:* A 500-foot-high dune nearly obscures Au Sable Point at sunrise.

Backpackers admire the view from a rocky spit in Pictured Rocks National Lakeshore. *Below:* Cheerfully rustic cabins provide lodging for winter visitors in nearby Munising. *Opposite:* Chapel Falls at Pictured Rocks National Lakeshore carry the first autumn leaves downstream.

Preceding page: Giant icicles curtain this February view of Lake Superior from an ice cave on Grand Island in Hiawatha National Forest on the Upper Peninsula. *This page, above:* Snow blankets East Channel Lighthouse in the Hiawatha National Forest, a stark reminder of a bygone era. *Below:* Ice fishing houses stand amid a world of white on Munising Bay, Lake Superior.

Big Bay Point Lighthouse stands dramatically against a sunset sky. *Below:* Midsummer flowers glow with color along a street in Kearsarge on the Keweenaw Peninsula.

Copper and iron mining once dominated the Upper Peninsula's economy. An old copper mine in Hancock (above, left) rusts in a range of vivid colors. Millions of tons of copper ore once rose to the surface in Hancock's Quincy Mine #2 Shaft House (right). *Below:* A onetime mining camp residence stands in the town of Central.

The restored buildings in Fayette Historic State Park illustrate an early iron-manufacturing village. *Below:* This picturesque Fayette ruin was once an iron smelter.

and fishing. Along the upper western side of the Lower Peninsula lies Sleeping Bear Dunes National Lakeshore, a spectacular expanse of sand that shifts over a base of glacial rubble. The dunes sometimes rise over 400 feet in height. The park's name comes from an Ojibway legend, in which one particularly large dune represents a sleeping mother bear; North and South Manitou Islands out in Lake Michigan are her cubs. Pictured Rocks National Lakeshore on the Lake Superior shore of the Upper Peninsula offers a spectacle of a different kind: lakeside caves scooped from the sandstone by the pounding of wind and water. According to myth, the warrior Hiawatha created them by hammering on the rocks with his fists.

In each period of its history, Michigan has shown a different face to its settlers and its visitors. Traces of each of the state's past phases remain today. Wild lands like those that flourished before the arrival of Europeans are preserved in state and national parks. Here and there—at Hartwick Pines State Park, for instance—a stand of magnificent pines like those the loggers took down still soars skyward. Immigrant communities have their distinctive looks, sounds, aromas. The nineteenth century lives on in a hundred museums and recreated villages. Cherry orchards bloom in spring along the state's Lake Michigan shore. Despite all the changes through which it has come, Michigan still lives up to its motto, which translates from the Latin as "If you seek a pleasant peninsula, look about you."

Top: Brilliant autumn color beckons visitors across the Black River Bridge in the Black River Recreation Area of the Ottawa National Forest. *Right:* Black River reflections in early fall.

Preceding page: Maples blaze with seasonal color in Ironwood's Curry Park. *This page:* Lake of the Clouds in Porcupine Mountain State Park becomes a glassy island amid a sea of autumn hues in this pre-dawn view from the Escarpment Trail. *Following pages:* A Lake Superior sunset.

Index of Photography

TIB indicates The Image Bank.

Page Number	Photographer	Page Number	Photographer
3	Gerald Brimacombe/TIB	32-33	Terry Donnelly
4-5	Andy Caulfield/TIB	34 (2)	David F. Wisse
6 Top Left	Andy Caulfield/TIB	35 (2)	Steve Dunwell/TIB
6 Top Right	Audrey Gibson	36 (2)	David F. Wisse
6 Bottom	Andy Caulfield/TIB	37	David F. Wisse
7 (2)	Mark E. Gibson	38	Steve Warble
7 Bottom	Andy Caulfield/TIB	39 Top Left	Wayne N. Bronner
8 (2)	Andy Caulfield/TIB	39 Top Right	Mark E. Gibson
9 (2)	Gary Crallé/TIB	40 (2)	Mark E. Gibson
10	Bullaty/Lomeo /TIB	41	Greg Ryan-Sally Beyer
11	William Rivelli/TIB	42 Top	Michael Shedlock
12	Mark E. Gibson	42 Bottom	Louis Borie/ Photo/Nats
13 (2)	Andy Caulfield/TIB	43	Michael Shedlock
14 Top	Lisl Dennis/TIB	44 (3)	Greg Ryan-Sally Beyer
14 Bottom	Henry Ford Museum & Greenfield Village	45 (2)	Greg Ryan-Sally Beyer
15 Top	Mark E. Gibson	46	Philip Schermeister/ PHOTOGRAPHERS/ASPEN
15 Bottom	Henry Ford Museum & Greenfield Village	47 (2)	Michael Shedlock
16 Top (2)	Mark E. Gibson	48 Top	Audrey Gibson
16 Bottom	Henry Ford Museum & Greenfield Village	48 Bottom	Michael Shedlock
17 Top	Mark E. Gibson	49 Top	David F. Wisse
17 Center & Bottom	Henry Ford Museum & Greenfield Village	49 Bottom	Greg Ryan-Sally Beyer
18 (2)	Mark E. Gibson	50 Top	Michael Shedlock
19	Henry Ford Museum & Greenfield Village	50 Bottom	Philip Schermeister/ PHOTOGRAPHERS/ASPEN
20	Greg Ryan-Sally Beyer	51 Top	Philip Schermeister/ PHOTOGRAPHERS/ASPEN
21 Top	Arthur Klonsky/Janeart, Ltd. / TIB	51 Bottom	Michael Shedlock
21 Bottom	Janeart, Ltd./TIB	52 Top	Philip Schermeister/ PHOTOGRAPHERS/ASPEN
22 Top	Frank S. Rodziewicz	52 Bottom	Greg Ryan-Sally Beyer
22 Bottom	Mark E. Gibson	53	Terry Donnelly
23 Top	Greg Ryan-Sally Beyer	54	Greg Ryan-Sally Beyer
23 Bottom	Sylvia Schlender	55 (2)	Greg Ryan-Sally Beyer
24 Top	John & Ann Mahan	56 Top	Philip Schermeister/ PHOTOGRAPHERS/ASPEN
24 Bottom	J. Madeley/Root Resources	56 Bottom	Greg Ryan-Sally Beyer
25	David F. Wisse	57 Top Left	Kitty Kohout/Root Resources
26	David F. Wisse	57 Top Right	Greg Ryan-Sally Beyer
27 (2)	Jack Olson	57 Bottom	Greg Ryan-Sally Beyer
28	HMS Images/TIB	58 Top	Greg Ryan-Sally Beyer
29 Top	Lou Bowman	58 Bottom	Sylvia Schlender
29 Bottom	Mark E. Gibson	59 (2)	Michael Shedlock
30	HMS Images/TIB	60	Michael Shedlock
31	David F. Wisse	61	Michael Shedlock
		62-63	David F. Wisse